THE **BEST BOOK** OF

Wolves and
Wild Dogs

Christiane Gunzi

KINGFISHER

Contents

KINGFISHER

a Houghton Mifflin Company imprint
222 Berkeley Street
Boston, Massachusetts 02116
www.houghtonmifflinbooks.com

Created for Kingfisher Publications Plc
by Picthall & Gunzi Limited

Author and editor: Christiane Gunzi
Designer: Dominic Zwemmer
Consultant: Lisa Wallis,
   U.K. Wolf Conservation Trust
Illustrators: Michael Langham Rowe,
William Oliver, John Barber,
Bernard Robinson

First published by Kingfisher
Publications Plc 2003

10 9 8 7 6 5 4 3 2 1

1TR/0103/WKT/MAR(MAR)/128KMA

Copyright © Kingfisher
Publications Plc 2003

LIBRARY OF CONGRESS CATALOGING-IN-PUBLICATION DATA
has been applied for.

ISBN 0-7534-5574-9

Printed in Hong Kong

Meet the wolf

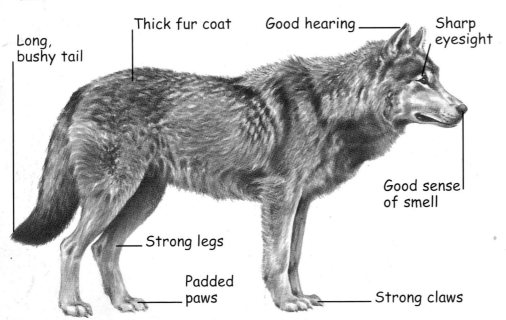

The gray wolf is the largest member of the dog family. Gray wolves, maned wolves, red wolves, and wild dogs are all meat eaters, or carnivores. Gray wolves and many other wild dogs live in large groups called packs. Wolves hunt mammals, including moose, caribou, and rabbits. Wolves once lived in many parts of the world. Today they are found in only a few places in the wild.

Long, bushy tail

Thick fur coat

Good hearing

Sharp eyesight

Good sense of smell

Strong legs

Padded paws

Strong claws

A gray wolf's body

Gray wolves have white, gray, brown, or black fur, and in the winter it is very thick. They have padded paws for running and strong claws and sharp teeth for hunting. Wolves have good sight and hearing and an excellent sense of smell.

Top dogs

Most packs contain up to 10 wolves. The pack leader is either the "alpha" male or the "alpha" female. In the spring and summer the wolf pack stays in one place, but in the fall and winter the wolves have to travel a long way to find food.

The alpha male and alpha female greet an older member of the pack.

Young wolves learn to fight by playing.

A world of wild dogs

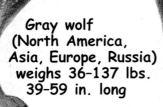

Wild dogs are mammals that live on every continent except Antarctica. They include wolves, foxes, dingoes, dholes, zorros, and hunting dogs. All wild dogs belong to the same family, which also includes domestic, or pet, dogs. Every domestic dog in the world is related to the gray wolf, which has existed for one million years.

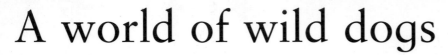

Dingo (Australia)
weighs 19–49 lbs.
28–44 in. long

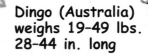

Dhole (Asia)
weighs 23–46 lbs.
35 in. long

Gray wolf
(North America,
Asia, Europe, Russia)
weighs 36–137 lbs.
39–59 in. long

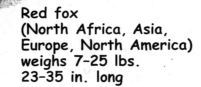

Red fox
(North Africa, Asia,
Europe, North America)
weighs 7–25 lbs.
23–35 in. long

Red wolf
(North America)
weighs 41–93 lbs.
37–47 in. long

Maned wolf
(South America)
weighs 46–52 lbs.
49–52 in. long

Coyote
(North America)
weighs 21–36 lbs.
28–38 in. long

Bush dog
(South
America)
weighs 11–16 lbs.
22–30 in. long

Golden jackal
(Africa, Asia)
weighs 16–34 lbs.
24–42 in. long

Summer
coat

Spring
coat

Arctic fox
(Arctic)
weighs 8 lbs.
21–22 in. long

Winter coat

African
hunting dog
(Africa)
weighs 39–82 lbs.
30–44 in. long

A change of coat

In the winter the Arctic fox's coat turns white to
blend in with the snow in the frozen Arctic where
it lives. In the spring the fox's fur starts to change
color. By the summertime its coat is dark brown.

7

The first wolves

Doglike creatures have existed for around 37 million years. Around eight million years ago a mammal called *Eucyon* lived on the plains of North America. *Eucyon* is the ancestor of all wolves, jackals, and coyotes. One of the first wolves was the dire wolf, which lived more than 10,000 years ago. This powerful carnivore probably hunted in packs. Its strong teeth could break the bones of mammoths and other prey.

Woolly mammoth helplessly trapped in a sticky tar pit

Gray wolf's ancestors

Dire wolves were only slightly smaller than the gray wolves that live in the U.S. today. *Eucyon* was about the size of a red fox. *Hesperocyon* was even smaller, probably the size of a cat.

Hesperocyon **lived around 37 million years ago.**

Eucyon **lived around 8 million years ago.**

Dire wolves lived more than 10,000 years ago.

Dire wolves in danger

Dire wolves roamed North America at the same time as mammoths. In ancient tar pits in Rancho La Brea, California, scientists have found thousands of dire wolf bones. The animals became trapped in the sticky tar pits and died there.

Hungry dire wolves, tempted by the trapped prey, stand on the edge of the tar pit where they will become trapped themselves.

Meeting and greeting

Wolves communicate with their bodies, their faces, and by making different noises. The alpha male and alpha female are in charge of the rest of the pack. They hold their tails up high in order to show other wolves how important they are. Less important members of the pack crouch with their tails between their legs to greet their pack leaders.

Happy   Playful

Frightened   Angry

A wolf's moods

Wolves make faces to show how they are feeling. A happy wolf keeps its ears up. A frightened wolf holds its ears flat. A playful wolf looks as if it is smiling. An angry wolf shows its fangs.

Alpha female being greeted by a less important female

Call of the coyote

Coyotes and wolves howl to tell other pack members where they are or to show rivals exactly where their territory is. Coyotes look like wolves, but they are smaller.

A place in the pack

In a pack every wolf has its own place, or rank. This means that some wolves are more important than others. The alpha pair are the only two that have young.

Coyote howling at dusk

A young wolf greets the alpha male by touching noses.

11

Growing up

The red fox is a beautiful creature with reddish-orange fur and a long, bushy tail.

Red foxes are found all over the world, particularly in Europe, Australia, and the U.S. They live in many different habitats, such as woodlands, deserts, farms, and cities. The gray fox is found only in North, Central, and South America. It likes to live in woodlands and can climb trees like a cat.

Gray foxes

1 A female gray fox gives birth to about four young in the spring or summer in a den under a tree or a log.

2 For the first few weeks the female feeds her young milk. Then the male brings the family food inside of the den.

3 For four months the cubs stay with their mother close to the den. She teaches them how to hunt for birds and small mammals such as mice.

4 After four months a young gray fox begins to find its own food. It hunts for prey and climbs trees to feed on fruit such as wild cherries and grapes.

A fox's den is called an "earth."

Happy families

A red fox usually has four or five cubs, and they are very playful. At two months old red fox cubs start eating earthworms, beetles, small mammals, birds, and fruit. Foxes like to bury their spare food, and they usually remember where they hid it!

The female red fox, or vixen, guards her cubs while they play.

13

Finding food

Most wild dogs, including wolves, are known as carnivores because they hunt and eat other animals. Some wild dogs, such as foxes and jackals, are called omnivores. This is because they hunt prey, but they also eat fruit, plants, birds' eggs, carrion, and food in garbage cans. Wild dogs usually search for food when it is dark—at night or in the early morning or evening.

Dingoes in the dark

Dingoes are the largest predators in Australia. They usually hunt at night, either alone or in pairs. Dingoes feed on rabbits and other mammals.

Dingoes chase a gray kangaroo at night.

14

Golden jackals scavenging for food in a garbage can

Garbage raiders

Jackals and foxes often live near towns and close to people. Early in the morning and at dusk these clever wild dogs scavenge for leftover food in piles of garbage. Jackals are very daring!

15

African hunting dogs

These colorful wild dogs live in packs on the African grasslands, where they hunt gazelles, antelope, zebras, impalas, and wildebeests. Hunting dogs never stay in the same place for more than two or three days. They wander through huge areas and travel hundreds of miles. These dogs take care of each other. After a hunt they bring back food to the sick, injured, and older members of the pack that stayed behind.

Baby-sitting
Pups stay in a den for the first four weeks. After the pups leave the den other adults will take care of them when their mother goes hunting.

The big chase
Hunting dogs look for prey in the mornings and evenings when it is cool. They hunt well together and can run as fast as 34 mph (55km/h). One dog leads the pack, and the pack will often chase an animal for several miles.

The pattern on every dog's coat is different.

A friendly pack

There are usually 10–15 African hunting dogs in a pack. Unlike some wild dogs, these dogs are friendly toward each other and usually do not fight. During the hottest part of the day they sleep and rest in the shade. When it is time to go hunting, they wake up, stretch, and greet each other with great excitement.

Pack of African hunting dogs resting

African hunting dogs hunting a zebra

Wild dogs of Australia

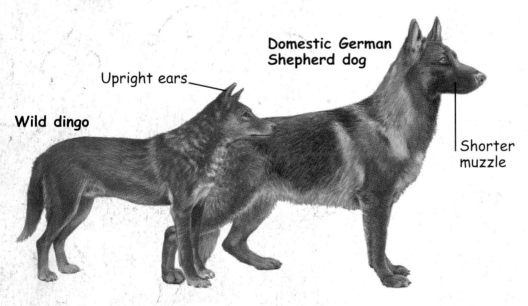

Dingoes are wild dogs that live in Australia, but they were not always wild. Thousands of years ago people traveling from Asia to Australia took some domestic dogs with them. Eventually these dogs began to live in the wild. In some parts of Australia dingoes are a nuisance to sheep farmers because they kill and eat their sheep. To keep dingoes away from the sheep there is a 3,100-ft.-long fence across Australia!

Upright ears

Domestic German Shepherd dog

Wild dingo

Shorter muzzle

Dingoes and domestic dogs

Dingoes belong to the same species as domestic dogs such as German Shepherds. A dingo looks similar to a German Shepherd, but it is smaller and has a longer muzzle. A dingo's ears are always upright, or pricked.

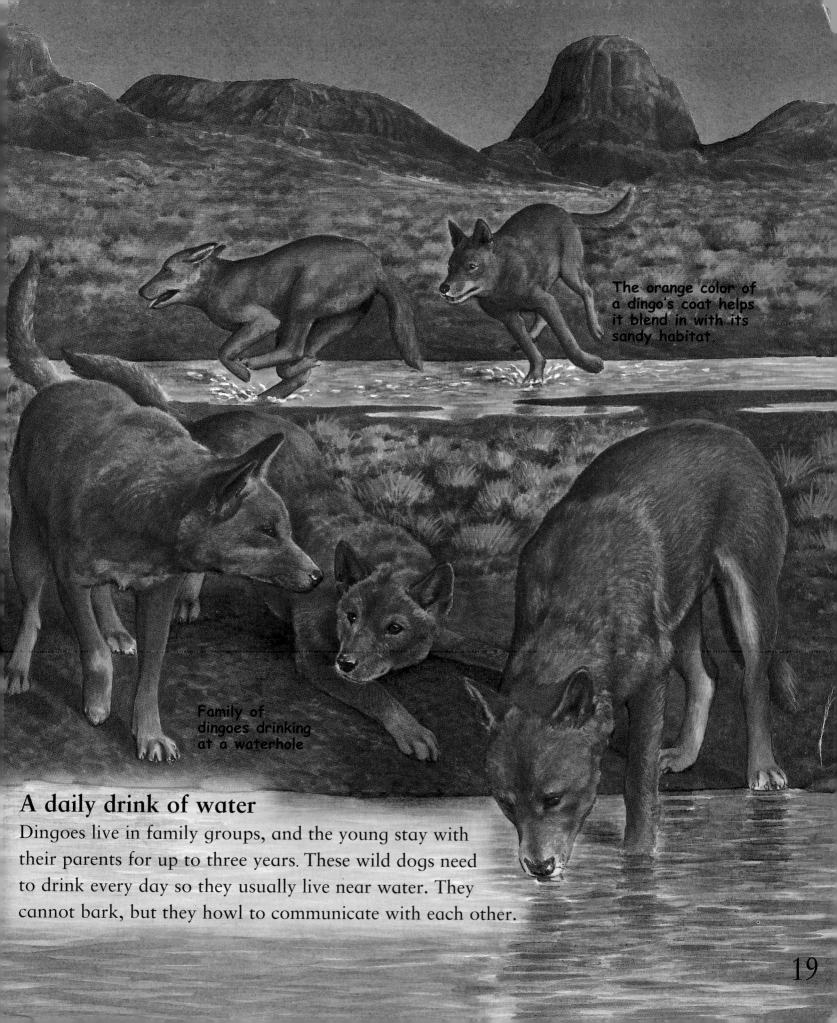

The orange color of a dingo's coat helps it blend in with its sandy habitat.

Family of dingoes drinking at a waterhole

A daily drink of water

Dingoes live in family groups, and the young stay with their parents for up to three years. These wild dogs need to drink every day so they usually live near water. They cannot bark, but they howl to communicate with each other.

Mountain dogs

High up in the mountains of Asia there are dogs called dholes. These wild dogs have existed for millions of years. Dholes prefer to live in forest areas, but they can also be found on open plains. They are usually seen in packs of around 10. Dholes like water and are very good swimmers. After eating they will often drink from a pool or sit in the water.

A dhole has a bushy tail, which it can wag just like a domestic dog.

A dhole's diet

Dholes are different from all other dogs because they have 42 teeth instead of 44. They eat all types of food, from large mammals such as guar and caribou to lizards, goats, hares, and even berries.

Guar (Indian bison)

Caribou

Lizard

Berries

Wild boar

Wild goat

Hare

All together now

Dholes usually work together when they hunt fierce and dangerous prey such as wild boar. Dholes also work together to care for their young. The adults in a pack help feed and guard all of the pups.

Dholes call each other by making a whistling sound. They also mew like a cat and cluck like a chicken!

21

Foxes of the desert

Some foxes live in hot, dry deserts. Their large ears help them keep cool. To hide from the heat of the sun they dig burrows in the sand. There is not much water in a desert. Some foxes get enough water from their food so they never need to drink. An Arctic fox spends its life in a cold desert. Thick fur keeps this fox warm and camouflages it as it hunts in the snow.

Fennec fox

These foxes eat lizards, eggs, rodents, insects, and plants. They are mainly active at night and stay in a burrow during the day.

Fox types

There are at least 14 types of foxes, and they are all different colors and sizes. The red fox is the largest, and the fennec fox is the smallest.

Red fox
23–35 in. long

Gray fox
21–32 in. long

Kit fox
15–21 in. long

Ruppell's fox
16–20 in. long

Bengal fox
18–24 in. long

Arctic fox
21–22 in. long

Pampas fox
up to 26 in. long

Bat-eared fox

The huge ears of a bat-eared fox help it listen for beetles, termites, spiders, and scorpions. It has sharp claws for digging and up to 50 small teeth for crunching tiny creatures.

The fox's ears can be up to 4 in. long.

A bat-eared fox shows her young how to pounce on a scorpion.

23

Racing jackals

With long, muscular legs and a lightweight body, a jackal is built for speed. Golden jackals live in the open countryside in parts of Africa, southeast Europe, and south Asia. Black-backed and side-striped jackals are found only on the African savanna. In some areas jackals are hunted by people. It is important to protect jackals and their natural habitats so that they can continue to survive in the wild.

Moving home

The side-striped jackal gives birth to as many as four cubs in a den. If there is any sign of danger, the female moves all of the young to a new den.

Jackals with black backs

Black-backed jackals often hunt in pairs, which makes it easier for them to catch prey. They eat small mammals, insects, and plants. Black-backed jackals also scavenge on carrion, or the remains of prey, left by lions.

Hungry jackal

Jackals are omnivores. That means they eat insects, birds, reptiles, amphibians, plants, and mammals, as well as carrion. If there is too much food to eat, a golden jackal hides any leftovers under a plant or digs a hole and buries the food. The golden jackal returns to its hidden food supply later when it is hungry.

Golden jackal burying a bird

Pair of black-backed jackals hunting for food at night

25

Lion's mane

A maned wolf has thick hair around its shoulders, almost like a lion's mane. It stalks mammals, birds, and other animals in the long grass and pounces on its prey like a fox.

A maned wolf can leap high over long grass.

A type of wild guinea pig, called a cavy, hiding in the grass

Amazing wild dogs

The tallest wild dog is found in South America and is called the maned wolf. Maned wolves are 34 in. high at the shoulder. They live in grasslands, savannas, and at the edge of forests. Each year the grasslands where they live are burned, so these dogs are endangered. The South American bush dog looks more like a bear cub than a wild dog, but it is a dog. Bush dogs live in rain forests and at the edges of savannas close to water. They can swim well.

Bush dogs leaving their underground burrow

Burrowing bush dogs

These carnivores live in burrows in groups of as many as eight animals. They have long, strong claws for digging. Bush dogs are good hunters and can catch animals bigger than themselves such as deer and large rodents.

Wild dogs in danger

The main threat to wild dogs comes from humans. For hundreds of years wolves and wild dogs have been hunted by people for their fur and meat and because they sometimes kill and eat farm animals. Today many wild dogs are endangered. Some, such as the African hunting dog and the Ethiopian wolf, may soon be extinct. In order for these animals to survive in the wild we must protect them and their habitats.

Wolves of Africa

The Ethiopian wolf lives on the grasslands high up in the mountains of Ethiopia, Africa, where it hunts for mole rats and other rodents. This wolf is so rare that there are only a few hundred left in the wild.

Fake fur, not fox fur!

Thousands of foxes and wolves have been killed so that people can wear fur. Now there are fake furs that people can wear instead. They even look like real fur.

Family of Ethiopian wolves playing

28

Small-eared zorro

This wild dog is a type of South American fox that lives in rain forests. It is an endangered animal because many trees in the forests where it lives are being cut down and burned. Parts of the rain forest are being cleared to make room for buildings and farms.

Clearing where rain forest trees are being cut down to make space for farmland

A small-eared zorro in its rain forest home

Studying wolves

There are only a few thousand wild wolves left in some parts of the world. The red wolf was hunted so much that it almost became extinct. Scientists saved the red wolf by breeding a few in captivity. In national parks in North America red wolves are being released into the wild. Today there are between 50–80 red wolves living in these parks.

A herd of caribou makes good prey for wolves.

Releasing red wolves

When red wolves are released into the wild, they wear collars with radio transmitters on them. These transmitters send out signals that allow scientists to keep track of the wolves.

Tracking gray wolves

In the cold forests in the far north of Canada experts follow packs of gray wolves by airplane. They check that the animals are healthy and make sure that they have enough prey to eat.

Scientists following gray wolves in an airplane

Glossary

alpha The first letter of the Greek alphabet. This word is used to describe the male and female leaders of a wolf pack.

camouflage The different colors and markings on an animal that help it hide in the wild.

captivity An animal that has been caught and is not free is in captivity.

carnivore An animal, such as a cat or dog, that eats meat.

carrion An animal that has been killed but has not been completely eaten by its predator. Other animals often eat the remains.

communicate Animals communicate, or talk to each other, by smell, by voice, or by the way that they stand or move.

continents Huge areas of land. There are seven continents: Asia, Africa, North America, South America, Europe, Australia, and Antarctica.

domestic Not wild. An animal, such as a dog or cat, that lives with people is said to be domestic.

endangered An animal or plant that is in danger of dying out forever. Maned wolves are endangered animals.

extinct An animal or plant that has died out forever. Dire wolves and woolly mammoths are extinct animals.

habitat An animal's habitat is its natural home in the wild. A gray fox's natural habitat is woodlands.

mammals Animals, such as dogs and cats, that are covered with fur or hair, give birth to live young, and feed them milk.

mane An area of thick fur around a lion's shoulders. Maned wolves also have a type of mane.

omnivore An animal, such as a fox, jackal, or bear, that eats fruit, plants, and eggs, as well as meat.

pack A large group of wolves or wild dogs is known as a pack. There may be dozens of animals in one pack.

predators Animals that hunt and prey on other animals are known as predators. Wolves and lions are predators.

prey Animals that are hunted and eaten by wolves and other predators.

rodents Small mammals, such as rats, mice, and squirrels, are rodents. They are prey for wild dogs.

savanna Huge, flat areas of grasslands in Africa with only a few trees. African hunting dogs live on the savanna.

scavengers Animals that search for and finish eating food left by other animals. Jackals are scavengers.

territory The area where an animal lives is called its territory. Wolves have large territories.

Index